*Author:*
**Peter Hicks** studied history at the University of London, Open University and the University of Sussex and is a certified field archaeologist. He has written many historical books for children.

*Artist:*
**David Antram** was born in Brighton, England, in 1958. He studied at Eastbourne College of Art and then worked in advertising for fifteen years before becoming a full-time artist. He has illustrated many children's non-fiction books.

*Series Creator:*
**David Salariya** was born in Dundee, Scotland. He has illustrated a wide range of books and has created and designed many new series for publishers both in the U.K. and overseas. In 1989, he established The Salariya Book Company. He lives in Brighton with his wife, illustrator Shirley Willis, and their son Jonathan.

*Editors:*
Karen Barker Smith
Stephanie Cole

Created, designed, and produced by
**The Salariya Book Company Ltd**
Book House, 25 Marlborough Place,
Brighton BN1 1UB

Please visit The Salariya Book Company at:
**www.salariya.com**

ISBN-13: 978-0-531-14606-4 (lib. bdg.)   978-0-531-16367-2 (pbk.)
ISBN-10: 0-531-14606-5 (lib. bdg.)   0-531-16367-9 (pbk.)

All rights reserved.
Published in 2002 in the United States by Franklin Watts
An imprint of Scholastic Inc.
557 Broadway, New York, NY 10012
Published simultaneously in Canada.

A CIP catalog record for this title is available from the Library of Congress.

Printed and bound in Shanghai, China.
Printed on paper from sustainable forests.
Reprinted in 2011.
16 17 18 19 20 R 12 11

# You Wouldn't Want to Live in a Wild West Town!

Written by
**Peter Hicks**

Illustrated by
**David Antram**

## Dust You'd Rather Not Settle

Created and designed by
**David Salariya**

**W**
## FRANKLIN WATTS
A Division of Scholastic Inc.
NEW YORK • TORONTO • LONDON • AUCKLAND • SYDNEY
MEXICO CITY • NEW DELHI • HONG KONG
DANBURY, CONNECTICUT

# Contents

# Introduction

After the Civil War (1861–1865) ended, the Great Plains were opened up. Cowboys herded millions of cattle across these vast expanses of grassland west of the Mississippi River. Farmers tried to grow crops on the plains, and hunters killed the buffalo that grazed on them. This was a dangerous place to be. The Plains Indians — Sioux, Crow, Pawnee, Cheyenne, Comanche, and Kiowa — fought hard to protect their land. People suffered in the heat of the summer and froze in the winter. Soon settlements sprung up. They began with just a few ex-army tents selling basic supplies. If they were in a good spot, they became towns, providing goods and services for the men trying to make a living. Life in these towns was often uncomfortable and violent. They attracted all sorts — the good, the bad, and the wild. Your name is Jim McGuire, and you are the marshal of a town called Dustville. You are more than qualified to understand why you wouldn't want to live in a wild west town!

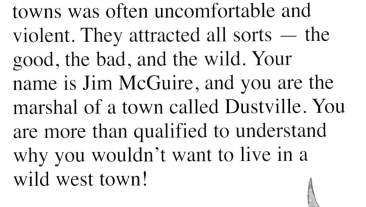

# Welcome to Dustville!

Early one morning, you take a stroll down Main Street in Dustville, the place you call home. Main Street is the busiest part of town. There is a whole range of businesses here, from shops and hotels to theaters and taverns. The storekeepers can supply you with clothing, boots, groceries, saddles, pistols, rifles, ammunition, and even haircuts! Everything for the farmer, cowboy, buffalo hunter, traveler, cattleman, or townsman can be found here. Remember to tip your hat politely to the town mayor when you pass him — after all, he is your employer!

As usual, you try hard to ignore the dust everywhere. During dry spells nothing stops it from flying. Horses, wagons, and the stage coach make it worse, and it lands on everybody and everything.

**Handy Hint**

Avoid making eye contact with strangers. They might think you're looking for a fight!

Morning, Mayor!

# Look Out – Stampede!

Jingle

THE LONGHORN is a tough breed. They can be any color and weigh 800–1000 pounds. The horns can reach 8 feet (2.5 m) end to end!

250,000 longhorns pass through the cattle pens in Dustville every year. It's a very big business.

TRAINS carry the cattle from Dustville to Chicago, their final destination.

Turning a corner, you walk straight into a trail herd that has just arrived in town! It is a herd of longhorn cattle that cowboys have driven up from Texas. They are noisy, dangerous, and smelly — and that's just the cowboys! In Texas longhorns are worth $4 each. In the northern cities they sell for $40, and this trade makes Dustville prosperous. Longhorns are unpopular with local farmers because of the "Texas fever." This contagious disease is carried by longhorns, and it could wipe out the local cattle. The longhorns are kept away from local farms.

Yikes!

YELP!

# The Cowboys Are in Town!

## What They Wear:

A WIDE-BRIM HAT as protection against the sun, rain, and snow.

A KNOTTED HANDKERCHIEF for use as a breathing mask, bandage, and water filter.

A LEATHER VEST for keeping safe a watch and money.

A HOLSTER AND GUN BELT. Not all cowboys wear these. Guns and ammunition are expensive.

LEATHER BOOTS. They are good for protection but difficult to walk in.

LEATHER CHAPS to protect their legs from bushes, thorns, and cattle horns.

SPURS to speed up their horses.

No sooner have the cattle noisily passed by than the cowboys who have just herded them up start to cause trouble. These men have been in the saddle for two months, and they've just been paid. You are called in to stop an argument over money, and you nearly get your head knocked off in the process! These men deserve their pay of $60 for the hard work, danger, and boredom of the last eight weeks. They have faced wind and rain, and have rescued their cattle from quicksand, mud, and barbed wire. They have been shot at by unfriendly farmers and lived on a diet of beans, bacon, and biscuits. All they want now is a bath, a shave, a haircut, clean clothes, and a good meal. Then they will go out and enjoy themselves, although some might get a little bit out of control...

# Hunting Buffalo

**Y**ou stop to greet two blood-soaked friends who have just returned to town with a bulging wagon full of buffalo skins. The nearby plains are teeming with buffalo, and good money is to be made from killing them. Their skins are sold for $3 each and made into leather.

The trade is not without its risks, though. Buffalo are very nervous animals, and stampedes are common. Since the hunters are killing the main food supply of the Plains Indians, the tribes often attack.

## The Buffalo Hunt:

SHOOTING. Buffalo hunters use a heavy .50 caliber rifle with a range of 600 yards.

SKINNING. Captured buffalo are skinned where they fall. Teams use mules to help in this gruesome process.

TROPHIES. There is a great demand for buffalo trophy heads. Many stores in Dustville sell them.

BONES. The plains are becoming full of carcasses. The meat is wasted because hunters only want the skin. The bones are collected and used for sugar refining and fertilizers.

13

# Law and Order

## Weapons:

Many shops in town sell the latest pistols and rifles. They're not cheap, however.

Dustville has a reputation for being a rough and violent town, and it is your job to uphold law and order. It's always worse when the cowboys are in town. Fights often break out over money. Sometimes townspeople have to dodge the bullets!

Run for your life!

LYNCHING. Sometimes hated criminals are broken out of jail by a mob taking the law into their own hands. They are strung up from the nearest tree.

Handy Hint

If you're caught in a gunfight, hit the ground fast!

Oh, no. My new shirt's ruined!

# Boot Hill

unfights are becoming more and more common. So many people are dying in gunfights that a new place has to be found to bury them all. You decide to use a rocky, craggy hill just west of town. Nothing much grows on it, and it drains well because it is a hill. The burial ground is called Boot Hill. A local shopkeeper doubles up as the undertaker when someone is killed.

He builds a quick pine coffin, puts it on his hearse, and takes it to the waiting grave, freshly dug by the gravedigger. If the dead person is a famous outlaw, he has his picture taken right in the coffin.

If you want to avoid gunfights, encourage visitors to hand in their guns at the jailhouse. They will get it back when they leave town.

Say cheese!

The outlaw is the best looking one!

BOOT HILL is the name given to the new cemetery because men killed in gunfights always die with their boots on.

A WOODEN CROSS, if anything, is all that marks the graves.

# Sickness and Disease

## What You Might Get:

**SCURVY.** This is a common disease resulting from a poor diet and lack of vitamin C. It makes your gums bleed and your teeth fall out.

Y ou have a terrible toothache, but there is no proper dentist. You decide to visit the blacksmith instead, but you soon wish you hadn't! Health is a problem in Dustville. It is not a clean place, and the death rate from disease is high. There are no sewers, so you make do with cesspits, which overflow when it rains. Flies are a constant problem because of the large amount of manure dropped by the longhorns. Infections spread easily. Also, the first doctors in Dustville are not well trained. They make mistakes, and many people die.

stinky skunk

**TUBERCULOSIS** is an infectious disease of the lungs. The symptom is a continual cough that often brings up blood.

Shiver

Take it away!

**CHOLERA** is a deadly disease, usually spread by infected water.

**RABIES** is a very serious disease, spread by skunks who bite people while they sleep. Most people die from it, and survivors are often brain damaged. Sufferers have a fear of water.

# Indians!

Dustville today is very tense. A party of Cheyenne Indians has come into town to make some complaints. Sitting down with them and listening carefully, you can understand why they are angry. A recent treaty gives the local Cheyenne, Comanche, and Kiowa tribes the sole hunting rights north of their territory as far as the Dust River. However, white hunters tempted by the high prices of buffalo skins have been crossing the river onto their land.

**TEPEES.** The plains tribes are hunter-gatherers, so they are often on the move. Tepees allow them to set up and take down their villages quickly.

Handy Hint

If you're tempted to go into Indian territory looking for buffalo, don't go alone. You'll be killed in an ambush and never seen again.

**INDIAN ATTACK!** Angered by the destruction of their buffalo herds, Indians sometimes attack lonely farms.

**WEAPONS.** Steel has made traditional weapons like the tomahawk and spear even sharper. Bows and arrows are deadly. The war club, a polished pointed stone, has a long reach.

21

# Braving the Weather

DUST STORMS are a hazard in the summer. You can't see a thing, and the dust gets into your lungs.

FIRE is another danger. Fires are sometimes caused by lightning. Often, someone is just careless with a candle.

LAST WINTER was especially bad. Thousands of cattle were frozen to death in blizzards.

Dustville is very exposed to all kinds of weather. When it rains, Main Street is turned into a river of slimy mud up to a foot deep. Shopkeepers provide long wooden platforms in front of their shops, and planks are laid across the street for pedestrians. The mud still gets everywhere. During the winter, blizzards pile up massive snowdrifts. This cuts off transportation for weeks on end, and food supplies run short.

HEAVE!

Handy Hint

If you get caught out on the plains in a blizzard, kill a buffalo and take out its intestines. Climb in, and its body warmth will keep you alive!

23

# Fun and Entertainment

## Your Choices:

PRIZE FIGHTS are popular in town. They are seen as a great opportunity for betting.

THE RODEO, a chance for cowboys to show off their skills, is a big deal.

HORSE RACES also take place regularly. Fast starters and sprinters fetch very high prices.

As evening approaches, you have to deal with revelers and party goers. For many cowboys, who have been working hard for months, Dustville seems like paradise — full of comfort, fun, and entertainment.

There are many theaters. The most popular one is on Main Street. Plays, concerts, and comedy shows all do the rounds regularly, with mixed success. Some cowboys make life very unpleasant for entertainers who aren't very good, and you often have to calm things down. Other activities reflect the outdoor life. Hunting is popular both as a sport and a source of meat. Dustville greyhounds are famous for their hunting abilities.

Handy Hint

Prize-fight organizers are clever. The authorities do not approve, so they only tell their regular spectators the time and place. A 4:30 A.M. start works well. You and your deputies will be fast asleep!

# Later at Night...

This is going to hurt when I land!

**M**any cowboys head for the dance halls in the late evenings. Lots of the hotels also have billiard halls, which are popular places for friends to gather. As the night progresses, things often get rowdy. Your evenings are usually busy enough just trying to keep the peace. However, some dance-hall owners take the law into their own hands and police the halls themselves.

GAMBLING is also common in Dustville. Many cowboys and hunters lose all of their hard-earned cash to professional gamblers in the taverns.

TAVERNS are the main cause of trouble in Dustville. Men gather in them to drink, talk, and chew tobacco. They spit tobacco juice into containers called spittoons. It's disgusting!

# You Meet Your End

You are a popular marshal. You are friendly, carry out your duties well, and never run from trouble. You are respected by the townspeople for doing a difficult job in dangerous circumstances. However, one day two cowhands hit town and start looking for you. They are threatening and fully armed. They tell anyone who will listen that you murdered their brother last year, and they're "gonna get you." You turn the corner and walk straight into them on the sidewalk...

IN A BLAZE OF GUNFIRE, you fall to the ground. You have been hit in the stomach. The locals look on in horror.

IT LOOKS BAD. "I've been shot," you groan, as two of your friends pick you up and carry you to the nearest doctor.

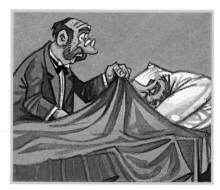

YOUR INJURIES ARE SEVERE. The doctor does all he can, but you die 40 minutes later.

AS A SIGN OF MOURNING, all the businesses in Dustville close for the day, and the shop fronts are draped in black.

YOU ARE BURIED at the mayor's expense in a little plot next to the town's chapel. Boot Hill is not for you.

LIFE MUST GO ON, and the mayor has to appoint your successor. After the funeral he pins the badge on the new marshal: your brother!

# Glossary

**Ambush** A surprise attack from a hidden position.

**Ammunition** Bullets or pellets that are fired from guns.

**Blizzard** A violent snow storm.

**Buckskin** Leather from a deer.

**Caliber** Width of the barrel of a gun.

**Carcasses** Dead bodies of animals.

**Cesspits** Holes dug in the ground to contain human sewage.

**Chaps** A piece of clothing made of leather and worn over pants to protect a cowboy's legs.

**Civil War** A war fought between the Southern states (Confederacy) and the Northern states (Union) of America between 1861 and 1865.

**Contagious** Easily spread by close contact.

**Cowhand** Another word for cowboy.

**Fertilizer** Material that makes the soil better for growing plants.

**Hearse** A vehicle used to carry dead bodies to the place of burial.

**Holster** A leather holder for a pistol.

**Lynching** The killing of a suspected criminal without a trial.

**Marshal** The chief peace officer of a town.

**Mayor** The person who is in charge of a town. He is elected by the people.

**Outlaw** A person on the run from the law.

**Plains Indians** Tribes of American Indians who lived on the Great Plains west of the Mississippi River.

**Quicksand** Loose, wet, deep sand that is easy to sink into.

**Refining** Removing impurities.

**Revelers** People having a good time and celebrating.

**Rodeo** An exhibition of cowboy skills.

**Saddle horn** The front of a saddle. Ropes can be tied to it.

**Sewers** Underground channels or pipes for carrying away sewage.

**Spur** A spiked wheel fixed to the heel of a cowboy's boot. It is used to kick a horse so that it will go faster.

**Stage coach** A horse-drawn coach carrying passengers to towns along a set route.

**Steer** A young male cow.

**Tepee** A tent made of soft animal hide stretched over long wooden poles.

**Trail herd** A large group of cattle driven long distances to a particular destination.

**Undertaker** A person who prepares dead bodies for burial or cremation.

**Wagons** Four-wheeled vehicles made of wood for carrying heavy loads.

# Index